Preface

The first time I experienced racism is when I was in kindergarten. I had a teacher that would always get on me or my friends that were black. We noticed when the white kids would do something the teacher wouldn't make a big deal over it. I said to myself at the time, "Let me pay close attention to the teach if she will say anything." For a week I watched over and over white kids would talk or do wrong things. The teacher never said much to them at all. When the black kids would do it then she wants to threaten us with phone calls home, after school detention or referral. The kind of child I was I would confront anyone that I had a problem with. I told the teacher that I noticed she makes a difference with the white children. She asked, "What do you mean?" I told her," When the black children do the same things as the white children we get into trouble. Why is that?"

The teacher couldn't believe what I was saying to her at such a young age. She looked at me and said, "They just aren't loud as y'all when they do things. Now go back to your seat." I knew that was a lie, but she stopped being so openly racist for a while. At that point I learned quickly that I was different due to my skin color.

Today, when looking to identify racism in this world one only need to follow the smoke. That's right the smoke. For centuries, where racism exists, fires have blazed both literally and figuratively. During the late 19th century, a lynching was the "go to" sign, as thousands of black men were hanged on trees and set on fire to burn at the stake. Today, while the black men may no longer burn, the shoes endorsed by many black men go ablaze. Why? Our White brothers and sisters may state it is about their fiery allegiance, but as you will learn in this book it is 21st century racism, our what we call in this book Passive

Aggressive Racism (PAR). Before we get into PAR, let us take a step back and to ensure we fully understand racism at its core.

Racism, as defined by Google Dictionary, is prejudice, discrimination, or antagonism directed against someone of a different race based on the belief that one's race is superior. The practice of racism by the original European settlers was a catalyst to the atrocities of slavery and genocide throughout North America. Using Christianity as a weapon, Europeans justified the maltreatment of Africans, Native Americans, and other people of color (POC)— who they thought were beneath them, by misquoting Biblical text (Colossians 3:22 - "Servants, obey in all things *your* masters according to the flesh; not with eyeservice, as men pleasers; but in singleness of heart, fearing God".) White supremacists consistently justify the past and present inhumane treatment of African people. From the enslavement of Africans to the Trail of Tears of Native Americans, nothing has been made right.

The system of WS is a well-oiled machine, built on a racial hierarchy. If you have White skin or can pass for White, you receive the benefits of WS—White privilege. Unfortunately, people of color don't qualify and, possibly, never will because those in power categorize us by our overabundance of melanin.

Black Americans fall at the bottom of the spectrum when it comes to opportunity and the pursuit of the American dream. Although we are the most copied group of people in the United States, we are the most envied and the most hated group as well. That's the part that doesn't make sense to any sane person. If you hate us so, then why do you want to be like us? Why does the majority become angry as we grow tired of direct and passive aggressive racism?

Most people avoid people they don't like or distrust. White supremacists will stalk people of color on social media, give their unsolicited opinions on Black issues, complain about Black traditions, and complain if we promote shopping at Black-owned businesses. And, the list goes on. It promotes a desire for Black Americans to live separate. These feelings are not due to hate but due to being hated. Caucasians refuse to eliminate the racist element out of their group.

We've been forced to watch White cops be a part of known hate groups such as the Ku Klux Klan, Alt-Right, Neo-Nazi, and Neo-Confederate groups. We watch our brothers and sisters murdered on national TV or beaten beyond recognition by men in uniform hired to protect and serve our communities. The Black community no longer calls law enforcement police officers, because so many are race soldiers in the system of WS. Many White people argue that White police officers kill more White people each year than Black people. While this is true, Caucasians love WS more than the people in their community. Caucasians should lead the protest extrajudicial killings of American citizens, who may or may not have committed crimes. We have a right to due process of law. Black Americans shouldn't lead that protest, but as we stated earlier, the assessment is Caucasians love WS. Until WS falls, we as Black Americans must learn how to navigate living under this oppressive system.

White supremacy has always shown itself in two forms. Direct racism is how the country was formed and operated for many years. From the trans-Atlantic slave trade to the civil rights movement racism was in your face. Black Americans suffered beatings, lynching's, rapes, arson of businesses or churches, bombings, voter intimidation, the murder of

Black leaders, J. Edgar Hoover's COINTELPRO and theft of inventions. It was nothing to hear of, or to see, a Black man hanging from a tree. It took many great brothers and sisters to stand up against White supremacist terrorism. Black Americans have suffered terrorism at the hands of White Identity Extremists and are experts in knowing the evils of WS.

The civil rights movement made great strides against the day-to-day suffering of Black Americans and institutional racism in this nation. We honor the positive work from the efforts of Martin Luther King Jr, Malcolm X, Rosa Parks, Elijah Muhammad, Medgar Evers, and many unnamed soldiers today. However, once our great champions fought and won the battle, White supremacists went back to the drawing board to win the war.

Because direct and overt racism was no longer socially acceptable, instead of allowing the KKK to lynch Black people those same racist men joined police departments seeking new ways to subjugate and control the *lesser* race. They planted drugs on innocent men and, often, killed alleged Black criminals because they were *afraid for their* lives. More educated racist became district attorneys and judges. This new form of terrorism was harder to prove because the narrative has always been that Black people, especially Black men, are lying, cheating, thieving murders. No one feels mercy or believes that Black people deserve due process or Blind Justice.

Ever since the end of the civil rights movement, passive-aggressive racism has been the way of the White majority. You won't find a Black person hanging from a tree. Instead, a cop will say he was afraid for his life, excusing his execution of an innocent Black child. Passive-aggressive racism is a term I coined to give an accurate description of how America works. Passive-aggressive racism means to covertly use WS to trick, deceive and dominate non-white groups in a passive-aggressive manner.

Another example is how blacks are denied business loans although lenders deny that race plays no part in denials. According to Forbes.com, financial institutions deny business loans to Black business owners 20% more than their Caucasian counterparts. Black children are put in special education because some Caucasian teachers don't care to teach Black children. They say special education helps Black children. We know it doesn't help our kids at all. A Caucasian ran school system have a school to prison pipeline for Black children. We have Affirmative Action laws, yet Black unemployment is always higher than Caucasian unemployment. Caucasians will say race has nothing to do with the disparagement in employment as well. The code in WS is to use Passive Aggressive Racism. That's why when a Caucasian says the N-word or presents themselves as a member of a hate group; they reject their fellow Caucasian. Caucasians are vocal against direct racism because it is not socially acceptable nor good for business. If a direct racist admits to loving WS, he or she breaks the code. That's why many Caucasians take issue with people like Richard Spencer or David Duke. Richard Spencer breaks code so they must reject him. If Richard Spencer would be the same way but practice his racism in a Passive Aggressive way his community would accept him. Black Americans must understand passive aggressive racism because it has us in a worse position today than during Jim Crow. This book is written to help Black Americans identify and combat Passive Aggressive Racism. Caucasian Americans can benefit from this book because it will help them identify Passive Aggressive Racism in themselves.

Many of my YouTube channel's White viewers have emailed me saying how my videos have stopped them from doing racist things. They now understand that any person who supports WS is a White supremacist.

Chapter One

Asking Threat Based Questions

Passive Aggressive racism is a reality for many in this country. I can only speak as an African American who deals with it daily. When you look at television, most of the commercials have Caucasians in it. If you judged America's population based on commercials you would think there wasn't African American, Native American, Hispanic, Arab, Asian or Pacific Islander persons that lives in our country. When you look at Fortune 500 companies, most leadership is Caucasian and male. Our law enforcement, even in predominately African American areas, is overwhelmingly White. From police officers to prosecutors to judges, when one enters the criminal justice system, it is a sea of White male leadership and authority. Are African Americans seeking the jobs or running for public office? They are, but equality isn't reflected because Caucasians love WS. I used all the examples to make a point. When an African American person makes the kind of assessment I made, most Caucasians will never tell the truth. White supremacists know that US institutions and systems benefit them. Unfortunately, they will never admit it. Caucasians will benefit the most. Instead of facing the truth most of them will use deflection tactics on a Black person who questions the lack of equality. Let's explore common responses from those that rather deflect to hide their enjoyment of privilege due to WS.

Can You Prove That Racism Exists?

First, that question alone is beyond insulting to hear as a Black person. It is rooted in privilege and WS. White supremacists that ask this question already know the answer. This question isn't raised to spark productive dialogue and educational exchanges. It is asked to have you prove something that is blatant while taking you away from the position of truth: calling out WS. If you answer such a question, the job of deflecting from WS is complete. Now you're discussing racism instead of WS. When we allow them to take control of the narrative we fail at presenting our position.

Remember, WS raised them to feel their opinions are always valid over yours.

Never, and I repeat, never allow white supremacists to take control of the conversation on racism. The oppressor can never tell the victim how he or she feels about being oppressed. Don't waste your time answering the question. Instead of subjecting yourself to the goal of the oppressor, remain focused on your narrative by asking them to prove that racism does not exist. At this point, you've returned to the place of offense, so you can watch them struggle on the defensive end of the conversation.

Some of them are slick and will try to answer your counter question with "Our country isn't racist because we had Barack Obama as president." Barack Obama is the "go to" to prove racism doesn't exist. Barack and Michelle Obama were called every racist name in the book. Barack Obama couldn't do a thing for Black Americans. When George Zimmerman killed Trayvon Martin, Barack Obama stated, "If I had a son he would look like Trayvon." White supremacists went crazy about that statement, yet many politicians stated the same words about crime victims. What's wrong with looking at a crime victim and feel they could have been your son or daughter. Identifying with victims shows your humanity to the world. Unfortunately, for many White Americans, it is hard to identify with a murdered Black male youth because WS has taught them that we are not human. In fact, we rank lower than dogs to them. During Obama's presidency, I reported over the years of racist making lynching effigies directed at America's first Black President. Still, White supremacist tell the lie that we live in a post-racial America. More Caucasians joined hate groups during the Obama years than under any other president. The maltreatment and disrespect the couple and their children received during the Obama presidency reflects the values of WS in the United States of America.

Another response is "Black Athletes are millionaires in this country. If we are so racist, why do Whites allow them to make that much money to entertain us?" The proper counter to that is to focus on who owns and coaches the teams. How many Black Americans own NFL or NBA teams? Why are most of the owners Caucasian? Roughly 70% of athletes in the NFL are Black. Why are most of the coaches., approximately 95%, White? Once you start hitting them with the truth, they must back off from that. You have more answers on your side to counter the arguments they try to present to deflect from WS. As a Black person, you must learn how WS works. Your life and livelihood depend on it.

Can You Prove I'm Racist?

Incidents happen in this nation all the time, especially on the job. We've all worked with them, that breed of Caucasian who is always short with Black colleagues. Occasionally, you overhear them using Fox News talking points when discussing Blacks and other people of color. No matter what, they always side with cops who kill Blacks. More than likely, if you have cross words with these Caucasian colleagues, it's about their inability to see the social injustice served to your community. The Black person may call them a racist. Accused racist Caucasian colleagues will act so offended that it looks fake. At this moment, said colleague says, "Prove it. Prove that I'm racist."

Fueled with every situation you've encountered in the office (see above), you give them the run down. Their response, "I'm not a racist because I support cops or repeat facts from Fox News." People like that believe that if they don't say the N-word that they are not racist. I don't have to say I hate you for you to understand that I hate you. If I never have anything nice to say about you, support people that harm you, and believe the worst about you, then I probably don't like you. Any person would get the hint. Dogs know when a person treats them nice or mean.

A white supremacist doesn't have to utter a slur for us to understand they don't like Black people. Don't be shocked when we call you out.

As a Black person, you must make your statement about their racism and move on. It's not for you to try to convince them of their racist behavior. They already know.

Let's explore one more question often asked by White supremacists.

How Are Blacks Oppressed in America?

Your response should be, "I'm oppressed and victimized living under a system of WS. People who look like me have the unfortunate reality of watching Caucasian cops kill Black people and go home to eat a ham sandwich. We watch the media make victims out of cops, who usually have a history of using excessive force or making racial slurs. We watched as Caucasians raised close to half a million dollars to defend Darren Wilson, the cop that killed Michael Brown for no apparent reason other than he was Black. The criminal justice system sentences Blacks to more time than any other race in this country. Black women hold more degrees than any other race, yet a Caucasian woman can get jobs over educated Black women. Caucasians are given business loans at a higher rate than Blacks. Abortion clinics in Black neighborhoods outnumber those in predominately White neighborhoods, with the same White communities having the benefit of nearby fertility clinics. No matter the economic status of WS can take everything from a Black person. There is no system to protect Black people if WS wants to do something to us. WS gentrifies our neighborhoods and Blacks must leave homes their families have lived in for generations. Show me any time in history where Blacks gentrified a White area. Every day in this nation we fear for our lives. We have a right to say we are oppressed and victims of WS. I don't support a victim mentality but support the acknowledgment by all

Black people to call out WS as the source of our victimhood."

If they still won't listen, asked this question, "Would you trade being a White person to become a Black person?"

Every question presented by people who justify racist behavior is to make you defensive. Don't allow it to happen. Always be aware of their sly and cunning ways as they will do what they can to maintain WS. Remember any person that supports WS is a White supremacist. Don't allow them to tell you that a KKK member is the White supremacist. They support WS more than KKK members. In many cases, KKK members are White Identity Extremist, who most Caucasians reject.

The next chapter we will focus on wistful statements used in Passive Aggressive Racism communication.

Chapter Two

<u>Making Wistful Thinking Statements</u>

Black people had to fight for every right they have today. Grudgingly bestowed, our freedom came at a price. We were enslaved, raped, discriminated against, and still suffer White supremacist terrorism that our government allows. I truly believe that those who celebrate WS and violence are inhuman because humans feel for others. Humans are remorseful when they kill another person. White supremacists feel it's their right to kill Black people, so they don't bat an eye doing it. What's worse is many Caucasians support the actions of police officers. How does a person who is not a cop get away with killing a Black teen in cold blood? WS. Fox News gave George Zimmerman, the man who killed Trayvon Martin, a platform to spew hate and to present himself as a victim. According to the

Washington Post article posted April 27, 2012, Caucasians raised more than $204,000 for Zimmerman's defense on crowdfunding sites. Initially, we were amazed at the fact Caucasians would ban together to support a man who killed a child. Any person with human decency can view many in this country as straight savages. Black people have always formed groups to defend and stand up for our rights. We are a people that are always under attack on many fronts. The government killed many of our great freedom fighters because they desire to keep us in a slave like position. J. Edgar Hoover created the COINTELPRO (Counter Intelligence Program) to destroy equality and equity movements led by Blacks. The FBI and local police killed or jailed many of our leaders. The leaders who could, fled the country to avoid jail or death. We are the only race in America that the US government won't leave alone. Groups like Nation of Islam, New Black Panther Party, Urban

League, and National Action Network --to name a few--are needed in our community to fight for our rights.

Many white supremacists make wistful thinking statements against Black people have groups to defend our very lives. Wistful Thinking as defined by Google Dictionary as the formation of beliefs and making decisions according to what might be pleasing to imagine instead of by appealing to evidence, rationality, or reality. It is a product of resolving conflicts between belief and desire. We have suffered White supremacist terrorism for close to 500 years. Still, Caucasians don't understand or don't want to understand our need to unify as a community. Most Black people would like to live their lives like everyone else. We can't do that being under siege constantly in this nation. Thinking your life is over when you're pulled over by a police officer is no way to live.

It further aggravates our plight when Caucasians have the nerve to be offended because we, people who have suffered at the hands of WS and institutional racism, use the law to fight for our rights, our lives. Now, we'll cover common wistful thinking statements white supremacists use to try to make Black people feel the need to defend the groups who defend their lives.

If White People Had Groups Like Black Lives Matter or the NAACP, You'd Have a Problem with It.

This common statement is used to make you feel ashamed and to goad you into defending our need to have organized groups that fight for civil rights. Black people and other people of color are incapable of being racist in the United States. The majority population, Caucasians, don't have to defend their civil rights because their skin color grants them every right and privilege under the Constitution. There was a time when Black people were only counted as 3/5 of a person. With this knowledge, how could anyone believe that Black people could exclusively prevent White people in the United States from the pursuit of life, liberty, and justice? It is utterly impossible.

The only thing the Black community can do is name call based upon race. That isn't power. Calling a collective group of oppressors out of their names does little to their psyche or well-being as the story told is *his*tory—they, White Supremacists, create and coin the narratives as well. In the grand scheme of American politics and economics, the words of African Americans are close to powerless.

However, when white supremacists resort to name calling, it is a pull to the narrative set by them to castigate and oppress people of color. The power to back up the words is there, even if it's just a reminder of the historical significance of the words used in context to slavery, oppression, and, often, rape. White supremacists need no groups to defend them because the Constitution gave them rights and the US Government defends such rights. The power of WS extends beyond US borders to the world.

Black people and most people of color have no system to defend them from the clutches of the seeds of colonization. So, for a white supremacist to say, "I wish we had groups like that" further displays White privilege and deserves a response that checks them on the spot.

To check them you must inform them of how power, privilege, and system of WS upholds them. We should understand that most White people run on autopilot in their responses to Black people. Don't be afraid to challenge them to think, and to think differently. Your engagement may not change their minds, but it will give them something to think about.

Also, being open, candid, and willing to state your case lets them know you are not docile. White supremacists should know how important it is to be educated and informed by something other than Fox News when they step to you in conversation. Giving them the real version of their history and not propaganda is often enough to shut them up.

I Wish We Had the Same Privilege as Blacks to Say What We Want.

When you hear this statement, it's usually about the use of the N-word. The slave master created the term to demean and dehumanize us. It helped them to justify their maltreatment of slaves and to break the will of the men and women they stole from Africa. The slave master passed on this word to their children and their children's children. In private, the word is still used by many of them today. If you think otherwise, you're sadly mistaken.

Many of them teach their kids that word when they can barely speak. I have covered many news stories of Caucasian children saying the N-word to Black children or adults. It's sad to see them ruin their kids in this manner. Teaching hate is child abuse. The children taught to hate others are ruined before they get a proper start in life. I've seen many videos online where the use of the N-word by white supremacists cost them their job or business. Many of them don't like the social consequences of job or business loss. Many of them remember when they could say the N-word with no consequence.

The issue they take with Black people using the N-word amongst themselves in music and art stings because when we use it the power of the word wanes. When Caucasians use it, it infuses the power to demean and dehumanize. When Black people use the N-word, it has no social consequence for us.

Black Americans didn't steal White people from their homes and subject them to torn families, death, disease, poor working conditions, and enslavement for 246 years. We never freed slaves, after a bloody civil war, with nothing in the means of provision nor rights. We never practiced Jim Crow for another 100 years while burning down the homes and businesses of Caucasians. Black police officers aren't constantly killing Caucasian men, women, and children. We could never catch up to the evil White supremacist terrorist have done to us.

As a Black man, I don't advocate for the use of the N-word by anyone. I don't care if the N-word ends with an "a" or hard "er," it should never be used. Some of my brothers and sisters use the N-word, but it is not the same as Caucasians using it. Many Blacks died at the hands of slave masters, overseers, and cops with that being the last word they would ever hear. Caucasians will never have the right to say the N-word in public without social consequences.

I don't care how much many of them like Trump, we aren't going back to the past. We all supposedly have freedom of speech, so say whatever you will within reason. It's not against the law to use the N-word. Just don't cry when you're hit with the social consequences. From my perspective, WS is more important than food. The practice of racism and WS is more important than providing food for your family when you can't refrain from publicly using racial slurs. Jobs are hard to come by and to lose one over your need to be oppressive is dumb.

How Can You Afford to Live In That Neighborhood? Wish I Could Live There.

The motivation behind that statement is they're genuinely shocked that you as a Black person can afford something that they couldn't. WS leads Caucasians to believe that Black people should be poor and destitute. It leads them to believe that all Black people live in high crime areas with no hope for the future. White supremacists love to hear about Black people suffering because they measure their self-worth on their superiority to us. When a Black person does well in life, or better than them, white supremacists feel less than human. WS can't thrive with Black excellence, so White supremacist do everything possible to prevent it. Why do you think Caucasians rush to offer money to upcoming Black business owners? They know if the Black companies match them they are done. If Black people could provide jobs for our community, what good would Caucasians be to us at that point? They know this, so they seek to stop Black excellence. In the entertainment industry, WS promotes the most degenerate behavior among Black people. Sure, they pay the artist or reality TV star but inflicting damage on the Black community is worth the coin. American pop culture follows celebrities and mimic what they say, do, or promote. How many young ladies want to imitate Cardi B? How many young men want to be like 21 Savage? Even the name 21 Savage is problematic, but you get my point. Black degeneracy is how White supremacists inhibit Black excellence. Black people that exhibit Black excellence in business are singled out and purchased by White supremacist. The result is that Blacks stay in the slave position, owning and producing little if anything. WS wants us in a position of lack and dependency.

Many Black people exhibit Black excellence in spite the odds, and White supremacists dislike successful Black people. White supremacists can't stand to see or hear of a Black person having millions of dollars. They also can't stand when we are business owners, and money is no object to us. At that point, they look at themselves as a waste of White. White supremacists know the system is for them and against Blacks. Blacks outshine them, and it fills them with envy, jealousy, and outrage.

As the tide changes, more Black people become successful in this nation. However, there was a time when White supremacist set price points to keep Black people out. Now, some Black people are in a place where no price point is a limit for them.

As we watch WS slowly crumble, the feelings of despair have caused many of them to turn to opioids. WS isn't taking care of them like it used to. When I studied what was causing the opioid usage in the Caucasian community, it pointed to one thing: WS can't afford to guarantee them jobs without proper skills or education. The world is very competitive and being White is no longer enough.

Trust me; white supremacists don't like to see Black families move to prestigious areas. Blacks don't belong there. They must be aware that although the chips are stacked against us, we continue to pull ourselves up by the bootstraps. We can afford to live in any neighborhood now. Don't get mad at us get mad at yourself for thinking your skin would guarantee jobs for you or your family. Black people had no guarantees, not even the comfort of knowing where our next meal would come from. Some will say I'm Caucasian and I grew up poor. A poor Caucasian in America is still better off than any poor Black person in America.

Chapter Three

<u>Backhanded Compliments</u>

The purpose of backhanded compliments is to offer insults cloaked in kind words and niceties. The person wants you to think they're complimenting you when they are mean-spirited. I'd rather you come out and tell me you don't like me instead of you pretending to be my ally.

You must be a good listener, capable of reading between the lines, to catch backhanded compliments. Unfortunately, some people have a hard time listening for the real message behind words—they need concepts explained in direct terms.

Deception is a major component of WS and is one of the main reasons it is ingrained in American society since inception. When White people convince themselves and others the phenomena does not exist, WS festers and grows like the weeds in an untended garden. Have you ever noticed that when WS is mentioned most Caucasians in America play dumb? Some will go as far as denying the existence of or even ask "What is WS?" Don't respond because they know what it is and depend on it daily. WS only exists to oppress non-Whites.

As I study news stories involving WS, it amazes me that the practice of WS is life and death for them. They will risk everything just to be or sound racist. We will explore common backhanded compliments used as trickery for those who aren't paying attention.

You're Very Smart

Most people wouldn't question it if someone complimented their intelligence. "You're very smart," sounds like praise, an acknowledgment of your knowledge and wisdom. Remember, it's not what you say but *how* you say it. A person's body language, tone, and inflection are as much a part of communication as words. Did you notice the look of amazement and shock at the moment of realization? They are shocked and amazed at your intelligence because they form their opinions about Black people on ugly and baseless stereotypes. From their perspective, Black people are uneducated, a race of people that can't read or think for themselves. Believing this solidifies their position of superiority. Racist use the IQ test as the holy grail of intelligence. Even though none of them post their IQ scores, they claim to have a high IQ I've learned to flip that on them to the point it's a joke on my YouTube channel. When they claim to have a high IQ, we all laugh. Then we walk them through all the things wrong with the country and themselves. We inform them that the high IQ isn't working out too well for them or the country. Even the backwoods type racist feels they're smarter than Black people. I remember when I had a conversation with one of them about politics. As I broke down Dog Whistle Politics and mentioned the revelations of Lee Atwater to this White guy, he listened in shock and amazement, saying, "You're very smart." I don't let people get away with saying that to me. I asked, "Am I not supposed to be smart?" He was dumbfounded. Of course, he backtracked saying," I didn't mean anything by it I just don't hear too many Black people speaking in the manner you spoke"

Like the White man I discussed politics with, many Caucasians stick with stereotypes like a rat on a glue trap because they need someone to be less than them and they can rely on the media to report propaganda that destroys Black intelligence and humanity daily. Hollywood loves to show Black people in stereotypical television and film roles. Because of self-segregation and little interaction with

Black People, many White people have no real-world experience with how Black people and other people of color live.

Learning the cultures is important to me because it helps me to avoid stereotypes. When I speak to others, I have no preconceived notions of intelligence, employment, or other demographic factors.

I Didn't Like Black People Much Until I Met You

It amazes me how they think this is a compliment to a Black person. How are you going to tell a person you didn't like their race until you met this one Black person? Any Black person that would feel happy at that statement is what we call a coon. When we use the word coon, we are describing a

Black, White supremacist. My word choice is no mistake. WS is more the KKK or Alt-Right. The KKK, Neo-Nazi's and Alt-Right are extreme forms of White supremacists. A White supremacist is any person that supports WS. There are more White supremacists than those in the KKK or Alt-Right groups. Any person, no matter the race, can be a White supremacist.

The origin of the word "coon" is rooted in WS. The word coon originally came from a song called "Zip Coon" back in 1829. The song used the same melody as another popular song called "Turkey In The Straw." You may have heard this melody on ice cream trucks. It floored me when I learned that a melody from my childhood was a racist song. However, we took one of their own words to describe Black people who support WS. Most Black people are not Black, White supremacist, so we had to use a term to call out those who look like us but aren't for us.

We must understand the statement about not liking Black people until they met this one Black person is rooted in stereotype. The stereotype is all Black people are evil; so, be afraid of them. Many racists have no legitimate reason to hate Black people. In most cases, their encounters with Black people are so limited until they take one bad experience and apply it to the whole.

We must understand a sad truth, racism and White supremacist teach their children the same values. No child comes into the world hating people for the color of their skin. Instead of giving a child a proper education, family values, and morality they teach evil. It's not a child's fault they learned hatred, but it's something we must deal with as a people. As Black people, we are the experts in WS because we've lived the oppression and terrorism for almost 500 years.

It does not impress us because one Black person is all right in your eyes. We aren't impressed by White people not having racist attitudes toward our people because of one Black person. They can miss us with that BS because it's phony and fake. These insincere attempts at trying to get us to lower our defenses deserve the side eye.

You Speak Very Well

When white supremacists meet articulate Black people, it amazes them. It's kind of like the "you're very smart" backhanded compliment. The stereotype is Black people only use slang because they are uneducated. Black people must be bilingual. Don't be confused, the bilingual state of Black people is not speaking English plus another language. It is understanding English or a recognized major language plus the universal language used in our communities. We learn proper English in school so that we can navigate the educational system.

Note, people that are taught WS live in a bubble. They learn who Black people are through the television-Fox News, Hollywood films, and music videos. None of those things are indicative of all or even most Black people. Do we have people that speak with slang in the Black community? Sure, we do, and it's nothing wrong with using slang among the people in our community. I use slang from time to time in communication with my people. When I make news commentaries, I speak in a way for everyone to understand me. I am no English language expert, but I use what I learned in school to communicate with others.

Wow You Make A Lot of Money

The notion that a Black person would be financially successful amazes those that practice WS. The stereotype is Black people are poor and destitute. WS has done all it can to hold Black people in a position of lack and disenfranchisement. When the government released Black people from the chains of slavery, they went to do for themselves. Our ancestors couldn't ask Caucasians for help because segregation was the law. Our ancestors build self-sustaining towns, so they would not have to rely on the White man. Instead of leaving these towns to themselves, White supremacist terrorist sought new ways to terrorize Black people. White supremacist terrorists burned down or ran our ancestors out of the towns they built. After the Black people left, they would claim the towns for themselves. The Slocum Massacre of 1910 is an example of this. White mobs killed 22 people and ran the black residents out of town. Afterward, White people took the possessions of the fleeing and dead Black townspeople.

Still, our people found ways to prosper in the face of constant terrorism.

Although some of us are millionaires and even a few billionaires in our community, it pales in comparison to the number of Caucasian millionaires and billionaires. Of course, when a White supremacist sees a financially stable Black person, it blows their minds because a money-having Black person is rare. They can't understand how a Black person could earn so much money. Remember, since childhood, their families lied to them about Black people. Some of us are poor, but most of us are not. We can't be that poor when we're spending 1 trillion dollars a year. WS and Black excellence can't co-exist with each other. WS must have White people at the top and Black people at the bottom. Black success exposes that they built their system on lies, deceit, and fear.

When a Black person has money, Caucasians are the biggest pocket watchers. *Pocket watching* is when someone is counting or concerned how you spend the money you earned. With Black millionaires, White supremacists always ask, "What are they going to do with all that money?" They seldom question a White person about their money at all. They never question a White person because it's expected for Whites to have money. A rich Black person makes them feel inferior because if a Black has it and they don't there is something is wrong.

Never think it's a good thing for them to acknowledge how well you are doing financially. With the history of their ancestors, know that a White supremacist will try to destroy everything you build. The only time I have conversations with them is when they have money and are willing to share investment tips with me.

These backhanded compliments are only a few of the ones Black people encounter daily. There are many more we can cover, but this section is to encourage you to listen closely and read between the lines in conversation. WS is rooted in propaganda, misinformation, hatred, and oppression of non-White people. WS is the enemy non-White people. That's why I always use the term WS. It is a well put together system that has been destroying lives for close to 500 years. We must pay attention to all aspects of WS, so we can combat it every way we can. Always challenge backhanded compliments.

Chapter 4

Ignoring or Saying Nothing About WS

In the United States, we have come to view bullying as a horrible way to target, discredit, and make others feel worse about themselves. Bullying is horrible. At one point as a child, people bullied me at school, but it stopped when all of us would get home at night. I guess it was a little reprieve. Unfortunately, due to cell phones and the Internet, not only is bullying constant, it has the potential for bullies to humiliate their victims for the whole world to see. Cyberbullying is the worst.

Imagine watching a classmate being beaten or humiliated. You can step in and do something, but you don't. You just stand there. You feel bad, but you don't want to be the bully's victim. You don't want that wrath on you. You watch and don't report. When you do nothing, it makes you an accomplice. You're just as guilty as the bully. Part of you feels bad for the person. You may even try to comfort the person when the bully is gone. The fact remains you stood there and did nothing.

This is how White people who don't necessarily have racist views support the system of WS. This person sees everything that's wrong in the country—police brutality, alt-right, KKK, neo-Nazis, anti-Black propaganda, and a racial caste system. This person has the power to step in and do something, but they don't. Ignoring or saying nothing about WS makes them a co-conspirator with those who oppress us.

I know, standing up for the oppressed is easier said than done. However, it is necessary. I'll walk you through a few reasons White people stay silent about WS.

Being Outcasts in Their Community

White people understand there is a code in the White supremacist society in which they live, grow, and thrive. Even when a White person is not racist, they can't speak up for Black people. Why? Many of the leaders and decisionmakers in this country are White supremacist or White supremacist sympathizers. Due to White supremacists controlling the media, law enforcement, the criminal justice system, and politics, speaking up can bring devastating consequences. For example, if a White person speaks up for an abused or mistreated Black person racist Whites will retaliate to get said White person back in line. According to the Tuskegee Institute, the KKK lynched 1,297 Whites for daring to speak up or actively defend Black people. The White person could also be called names such as nigger lover, social justice warrior, or leftist scum. If a White woman violates the code by dating or marrying a

Black man, the woman is called a mud shark, coal burner, or, their favorite gender slur, whore. This rule for dating doesn't apply to the White man he can date or marry whomever he wants. The White woman can be removed from the community for her activism against racism and dating choices. The White man can be removed from the community for his activism only. A White person can also lose their life for trying to end WS.

For White supremacist, if they are not on top, then life is worthless. If a Black person is on top, then life is not worth living. They view a White person trying to end WS as a race traitor who must be stopped. Even though it's a risk, if non-racist Whites banned together, they could end WS in the United States.

White Supremacist Sympathizer

Another reason a White person will ignore or say nothing about WS is that they sympathize with the racist. The type of sympathy is not what most would think. The White person says," I know my cousin believes in the Alt-Right, but he's still my cousin." "I'm not a racist, but I agree what they're saying in a small way." "I agree with the Alt-Right, but I would never go to a rally." This type of White person is what you would call a silent honorary member of a hate group. They make donations to the Alt-Right, believe that any cop who kills a Black person has done the world a favor, and privately hope one day they will be courageous enough to stand publicly with their brothers. They support groups like Blue Lives Matter and consume most of their news from Fox News. When George Zimmerman needed money for his defense against murdering Trayvon Martin, they donated thousands to his GoFundMe campaign. The White supremacist sympathizer is the most dangerous group in WS because they hide within society, biding their time as they work in private to undermine the Black community. I'd much rather know who hates me than to live with, eat with, and trust someone who hates me.

White supremacy sympathizers always feel the need to tell others they are not racist but it's quite the opposite. If you're White and you find yourself agreeing with White nationalist and Fox News, it's safe for Black people to believe that you're racist. It doesn't matter if a family member is in the Alt-Right. If you're true to your non-racist principles, then it will show, and for sure you won't rationalize it. You won't find every reason in the world to say a police shooting is justified or automatically believe the police account. Anytime we hear you siding with the police; we already know where you stand.

White Privilege

White privilege is the greatest gift to White people. WS dominates and controls the world economy. No matter where White people go they are held in high regard. Propaganda, bribery, and murder paved the way.

People who understand WS sees the benefits for themselves. White males get better job opportunities and are given the benefit of the doubt when accused of impropriety. White women gain many of the same privileges. The scale tilts in their favor.

Whether rich or poor, white people know they can always find a White neighborhood with the best amenities and schools at their disposal. When Black people look for homes near the good schools, it's usually a White one because our neighborhoods don't have the access we want for our children.

Black people are forced to leave their communities to move into an area with people who don't want them there. If too many Black people move in, all the White people move out. The Whites aren't moving due to crime, dropping property values, or bad schools. They move because it doesn't sit well with them to be around Blacks. Even if the White person isn't racist at all, they still don't want to give up White privilege. They won't say it, but our common sense and their silence speaks loudly. White privilege is in the benefits package of a White supremacist system. Would you willingly give up your benefits?

It's clear that many White people will never speak out against WS. Therefore, Black people must stop asking or begging them to speak up for us. We should stop being surprised when we meet people who are racist. The system that's in place rewards that type of treatment. When they can kill a Black person and get away with it, it makes them feel powerful. When they commit crimes against their community and a judge sentences them to probation, that makes them feel powerful. The criminal justice system was designed for them, by them. White privilege means that even if you're guilty, you deserve numerous chances to get it right. When a Black person commits a crime, he or she is prosecuted to the full extent of the law. There is no second chance for Black people. We're given the maximum sentence for first-time offenses.

They know the racial injustice, yet they do nothing about it.

I'm tired of explaining racism to Whites. They have the memoirs, notes, and tapes of our great leaders who spoke out against racism. Let them read and see for themselves the atrocities of WS. If they don't get it by now, then its proof to us they choose not to understand.

I don't have time to sugarcoat anything to anyone. When White people collectively say racism is over, then it will be over. The fight cannot remain among just a few A few White people like Jane Elliot, who fought all her life to speak to White people about racism.

Racism will be the downfall of the United States if non-racist White people refuse to stand arm and arm with the oppressed.

Black Americans are considering relocating to other countries. Once Black people leave this nation, watch what happens.

Chapter 5

Leaving You Out

The system of WS reinforces the idea that the White race is the supreme race and must always remain on top. It is a system that oppresses everyone who does not look like them, having a pure dislike of anyone of African descent. The self-esteem of White supremacists increases or and decreases based on the condition of Black people. As long as Black people are suffering, poor, oppressed, crime-ridden, unemployed, and begging, The White supremacist is happy. The moment a Black person achieves any part of the American Dream, WS takes a hit, and the White supremacists become angry. History shows us what happens when Black people build successful towns. Places like Tulsa, Oklahoma, aka Black Wall Street, is a shining example of how White supremacists had to destroy Black progress. Many Black business owners were lynched for being accused of being uppity Negroes. If you're successful, then welcome to the club of uppity Negroes. White supremacists will always want to know how you got your money. They will ask you about your employment so that they can figure out your income status.

White supremacists love to pocket watch Black people. The "*pocket watching*" is relegated to them because no other race worries about the finances of Black people. Do you think they like LeBron James making millions of dollars a year? Do you think they like you buying a huge home in a suburban community? Leaving you out is a way to prevent your success. They must leave you out for their benefit. The points I want to cover are economic.

Jobs

Black unemployment rates are ALWAYS double that of Whites. In fact, black unemployment rates are often misleading due to the steady decline over the past few years it remains double our white counterparts. A racist would reason that the high unemployment rates for Black people are due to them being lazy. Like there are lazy White people, there are lazy Black people. However, if the White race is not judged by a few than why should other races, especially people of color, be judged so harshly? Laziness isn't race specific. White people look out for White people on jobs. It's always been that way. White people get in place and hire people who look like them. When there is a job opening, they tell their friends and family about it, putting in a good word to the White hiring manager. Even if there is a job posting, more than likely it's filled by another White person before anyone else knows about it.

Unfortunately, most Black people don't have that kind of connections. When we recommend other Black people for jobs, our White managers and supervisors overlook them for their White friends, family, and colleagues. I have personally tried to get other hard-working, experienced Black men with great work histories placed on jobs. Who was hired? An inexperienced, White guy. WS is quite blatant. How can Black unemployment go down when they overlook experienced Black people?

When Black people are employed, we must be more educated and experienced while working twice as hard as our White colleagues. It has been said that Black people are hired on their ability to perform, while Whites are hired to be present. Then, we are often paid less for this performance at or above our peers. Politicians would rather give Blacks low-income programs instead of jobs. Well paying, stable jobs are the key to providing a stable life for your family. In many cases, Black people create jobs for themselves and their community. If done properly, it is one of the best ways for Black families to build financial legacies for generations to come.

Home Ownership

Many Black Americans lease apartments or homes in this nation. Home ownership is something that every person should obtain. The lack of knowledge about home ownership keeps Black Americans in poverty. Home ownership is a financial asset. You can sell the home one day to make a profit. Leasing will only give you a leg up if you are leasing to own. Home ownership is also transferable, giving you the opportunity to gift it to your children. It also helps build credit.

White people own homes because they have been taught to own and they have the financial means through job opportunity to help them. The more money you earn, the higher your loan approval. We must educate ourselves on attaining wealth and property via homeownership. Unless it benefits them, most White people will not tell you how to purchase a home or save money. I will say if you have a White friend, they will put you on the game a lot faster than the collective.

Business Ownership

Business ownership is a way to be free from dealing with racism on the job. When you own your company, no one can tell you when to come to work. You don't have to ask for permission for a day off or take a vacation. You can purchase your private insurance to give to yourself and employees. The White collective doesn't teach Black people the steps to obtain business ownership. Why? Business ownership can bring financial freedom. Remember WS needs Black people to remain in bondage. They spent a lot of money and time into portraying us as less than. Anti-Black propaganda was used to make people around the world believe the worst about Black people. When you become a business owner, it nullifies the propaganda.

Imagine the feelings of a poor, White racist when they see you are a successful business owner. Imagine how they feel when the car you drive is worth more than their trailer. It hurts them to see you getting ahead and them living in the same trailer their grandmother lived in. To make themselves feel good, they assume you're successful because of affirmative action. To them, affirmative action is discriminatory towards Whites. Anytime I hear that I have a good laugh. How can Whites be discriminated against in a White supremacist system? No one tells that that success is due to government aid. So, they must keep this knowledge from you at all cost. They would rather you beg them for a job that they'll never give you.

Credit

Credit is a system in the country that everyone needs to know about and manage. Having bad credit can prevent you from getting jobs, cars, homes, and other necessities. No one pushes the importance of credit to Black Americans. Even comedians have joked about Black Americans having bad credit. When you have good credit, you receive lower interest rates. The lower interest rates will give you a lower payment and reduced payback on home and car loans. Having good credit is the key to your financial success. They never taught you this because it's not in the best interest of WS. Black successes will break down the social order for many of them. You can repair bad credit if you have the correct information. Find a great credit repair company to get you on the right track. Once you fix your credit, take care of it with your life. Never be in a position where you can't help yourself or others. Bad credit will cripple you.

World Travel

America has worked very hard to promote Africa as a horrible place to visit. They told Black Americans you will get Malaria there. The media always show the poorest parts of African nations. The fake news organizations will misrepresent the footage as truth. If I take my camera and go to the poorest parts of America, then post it as the representation of America I would be wrong. WS doesn't want Black people to go to Africa. Why? Black Americans spend over 1 trillion dollars a year. Most of those funds go to White-owned businesses. Black Americans spend millions of dollars on the sports, music and entertainment industries alone. If we listened to White racist and went back to Africa, the US economy would crash. All the talent would be in African nations bringing new economic freedom to Africa. They encourage us to stay and limit our travels and to stay away from the Motherland. We're not encouraged to get passports. They try to keep us so poor where we can't even think about traveling because travel broadens your perspective.

Find ways to travel using discount sites to save money on flights. Africa is a place where everyone goes except Black Americans. Many Africans want us to come to live and do business there. They rather deal with Black Americans over anyone else.

We must obtain our passports. It is as simple as going to your local post office for an application to submit along with your birth certificate, state ID, passport photo, and fee. That's all it takes to obtain a passport. Start traveling to broaden your perspective and because they hate it when we travel outside of the country. Don't let them fool you into thinking they would be glad you're leaving. If 50% of us purchased our passports, it would make the news.

White supremacists want us kept in the dark about money, jobs, the economy, travel, and politics. Instead of realizing it is better for everyone to be successful. They would rather us keep eating GMO foods filled with chemicals and preservatives. They want us to remain in schools here, so we can be further indoctrinated into accepting WS. Black people must focus on knowledge and information instead of name brand clothes. We must educate our youth that most celebrities and entertainers wearing naming brands are wearing them for FREE in hopes Black youth and young adults will set a trend and drive sales. It amazes me that most of the people wearing name brands don't carry the same amount of money in their savings account or even daily in their checking account.

Chapter Six

Sabotaging Black Progress

The system of WS can only exist with the oppression of non-White people. Therefore, all people of color are at risk. As stated in previous chapters, Black excellence is a problem for the White supremacist system, one built on lies and deceit. This system enforces the idea that Black people are inferior, a lie that has been at the forefront of their mission for more than 400 years. Any group or person that promotes Black progress is watched and stopped if their efforts are thought to be too successful. Remember, at the order of J. Edgar

Hoover, the FBI was instrumental in stopping a lot of our progress through the Counter Intelligence Program. This director sought to stop Dr. Martin Luther King, The Black Panthers, Malcolm X, The Nation Of Islam and many other groups. Before J. Edgar Hoover took over as FBI director, he stopped Marcus Garvey from his mission of taking Black Americans back to Africa.

Instead of helping, many White supremacists do whatever they can to impede Black progress. When we want to stay in the United States, it is an issue. When we want to leave that is an issue. I firmly believe that WS wants to hold us hostage. We must examine the methods used to sabotage us on a personal and group level.

Career

The reason for sabotage is to stop Black progress. The only way you will get their attention is if you're at a point of success. The only time White supremacist worry about Black people is when we are successful. When you obtain a high paying job, they will watch you because you shouldn't be there anyway. When you fail, they can say, "We gave a Black person an opportunity, but they couldn't do the job," or "The Black person could do the job but lacked integrity.

Be extra careful who you talk to or befriend on the job. No matter how educated or experienced you are, the White supremacist feels as though another person should have the job because affirmative action hired you because of your race. Notice, you're the only Black person in that position. It is lonely at the top, especially when you're Black and is always exciting when you see another Black person in middle or senior management roles. There is a sense of kinship and family at that moment.

White people don't understand it, and, possibly, never will. They seldom experience the sense of otherness that comes from being surrounded by people who don't look like them. Almost everywhere they go, they see White people.

The system of WS wants to make sure to keep successful, privilege lifestyles an all-white affair.

Learn everything you can about your company culture. Memorize the company handbook and follow the letter of company policy. If you have a minor infraction, you will be fired. A White co-worker can break every rule and be given chance after chance. I want you to learn the policy because if you're fired without cause, you can take them to court.

Years ago, I fell victim to one of their tricks years. I was naïve, but life is a learning experience.

The job was one of those "on call" positions, meaning if you received a call you had two hours to show up. The main boss in the department was harsh and seldom cut anyone slack. When they hired me, only three other Black men worked in a department of seventy employees. It was mostly an all-White male affair. Have you ever had a job where you felt they only hired you to stay in compliance with affirmative action? As I look back, I realize the department had more than a few racist White males. One day two of them sparked up a conversation with me about the boss. The conversation was something everyone was saying about how harsh the boss can be. I stated my piece, and they gave their opinions but guess who started getting the side eye. Me. One of the brothers overheard them telling the boss everything but left out what they said. It caused many problems, and the boss started looking for reasons to write me up. Long story short I was terminated. I lost a great paying job because I said the wrong thing to the wrong people.

Keep your conversation with co-workers to a minimum. Not every White person is that way, but you better screen them very carefully. Also, watch out for the non-White sellout. Sellouts are just like the White supremacist. Keep your conversation about the job only. Avoid discussing your personal life as well.

When you are Black, remember you are first fire and last hire. They sabotage us daily, and it won't stop any time soon.

Don't confuse blatant racism with you underperforming. I'm not saying that anytime you're fired it is because you're Black. Some people deserve to lose their jobs.

Destroying Your Character

The best way to sabotage a person's livelihood and success is to destroy their character. This is perhaps the most common, non-violent way White supremacist deploy their strategies. If your people don't believe in you or your work anymore, your progress towards success will halt.

Many Black leaders, whether in business or civic organizations, have their names dragged through the mud. If a leader speaks against racism, they are accused of hating White people. This accusation makes the Black person look bad in front of all white people even if the Black person is only speaking out against WS. All White people are not racist. If I were to make that claim, it would be inaccurate.

In addition to making false statements, White supremacist will stalk Black people who expose their hateful ways.

I've had several White supremacists join our members' only page just to hear what I was saying. The level of obsession they have with Black people is beyond human comprehension.

They also use the media to destroy the character of Black people. The media can make a victim into a villain. George Zimmerman murdered Trayvon Martin. When the media told the story, Trayvon Martin was the violent thug, and George Zimmerman was an innocent neighborhood watchman.

The media used every psychological tactic in their arsenal to make people hate Trayvon. The Trayvon Martin case made me realize that mainstream media is the enemy of Black people. We saw the same thing happen again with Michael Brown. The media demonized Michael Brown and made the cop Darren Wilson the innocent victim.

Martin Luther King suffered the same thing from the media. They painted a great man into a man that hates White people and adulterer. The media painted Malcolm X and the Nation of Islam as haters of Whites. Our civil rights leaders only wanted us to be free from racial terrorism.

The White supremacists thought we should have remained quiet when they bombed our churches, raped our women, and lynched our men. Even today, we should sit stoically when race soldier cops kill us unjustly.

They control the narrative, so when we speak up about the violation of our human rights, it is us hating White people instead of exposure of the heinous ways institutional racism harms Black people and other people of color. Of course, we hate the people who kill us. Who in their right mind would love a terrorist? White people didn't love Osama Bin Laden after 9/11. White people wanted to prevent that level of terrorism from happening to them again and went after Bin Laden. No one accused them of hating Arab people for going after Bin Laden. They received praise for finally seeking out a terrorist to destroy.

When we are terrorized and stand up for ourselves, they accuse us of hating White people.

I've learned not to listen when they speak. If you're not on the side of the protection of human rights, then I don't waste my time entertaining you. My time is precious to me.

Unfortunately, some Black people buy into character assassination tactics of White people. This type of Black person believes White is right and will believe anything White folks tell them about Black people. Instead of considering the source and looking into the facts, the White messenger is believed because of their whiteness. If White supremacists can convince non-racist Whites to believe that our champions for civil rights hate White people, then Black leaders lose allies. If the same White supremacists can convince Black people that our leaders lack character, they lose the support of the Black community. Halting Black progress is always the goal.

False Criminal Charges

Black people are exonerated more than any other group for crimes they didn't commit. The National Registry of Exonerations states "Black defendants are exonerated 2000 times since 1989." The criminal justice system is used to oppress Black people. In a previous chapter, we discussed how Black people are prosecuted to the fullest extent of the law when White people either get away with crimes or receive minimum sentences. When you make waves against WS, they seek ways to bring you down. One of the best ways is by convincing the public that you are a criminal. It takes long money to fight against a system not created for you. It takes even more when the people who are supposed to uphold the law see you as less than human. Guilty or not, false accusations will break you and lower your credibility.

Showing up in court is like receiving an invitation to an all-White party by mistake. White judge, district attorney, and jury. The only people who look like you are the ones in trouble.

Peaceful protesters are often taking to jail on drummed up charges. In many cases the goal is to charge and convict you of a felony, legally stripping your rights to vote, own a gun, or hold a passport. Make every effort always to follow the law.

Even if they can't find a way to bring criminal charges, the will seek ways to bring civil charges. Again, it's money you must spend. Losing money chips away at your financial stability and weakens your position as well as your character in the community. If it takes years, they don't care. Build relationships with great lawyers so you'll have back up when the time comes.

Whiteball

Whiteball is the equivalent of the word blackball, except that it refers to White supremacist efforts and ideas to keep Black people out of politics, employment, and financial stability. Black people don't have the power to shut out anyone from anything systematically. When someone is Whiteballed, they can't get a job in any industry because the word is out never to hire that person because she said person pissed off White folks. We will look at two recent examples of this happening.

The comedian and actress Monique had a spat with director Lee Daniels. When she won her Academy Award during her acceptance speech, she didn't thank Lee Daniels or the studio. Daniels didn't like that at all and confronted Monique. Monique didn't feel she had to do that or promote the film, *Precious*. Monique was paid $50,000 for her role in the movie, and she spoke out about that. Monique felt Lee Daniels went on a campaign to Whiteball her from Hollywood. Even if Lee Daniels wanted to do that, he doesn't own or control Hollywood. No Black person owns or controls it.

The word to Whiteball Monique came from the White folks who own Hollywood. Monique won an Academy Award and can't get an acting job to save her life. They sabotaged her career. Monique is well known and talented, yet she couldn't escape WS when it came for her.

The next person I want to focus on is Colin Kaepernick. Colin Kaepernick played for the San Francisco 49ers without any problems in the NFL. Colin Kaepernick started taking a knee during the national anthem. Reporters asked him why he was doing that. Colin told the reporters to take a stand against police brutality. It wasn't about a flag or White people, yet when it was all said and done, they used that to destroy his character. Colin was a free agent, and many teams needed a quarterback. The NFL owners got together to Whiteball Colin Kaepernick. Quarterbacks were getting hurt left and right during that season. The NFL owners told on themselves when they were getting players that retired or haven't played in a year or more. Although Colin was game-ready, they passed over him. Why? They wanted to send a message to Colin and the other players. The message was "stay in your place, or we take away your career." WS disregarded Colin's hard work and eliminated him from football. I was so disgusted that I boycotted the NFL by not watching the games or purchasing merchandise. I refuse to support a league that would be that racist, and I don't know why Black men play for them. If they did it to Colin, they would do it to them also. The only thing Black people are good for is to make money for them. They don't care about the lives of our people. Many Black people and other people of color have been Whiteballed as well. The system of WS wants to stay intact.

When a Black person gains financial success, if they help other Black people White supremacists will come after them. If a wealthy Black person speaks up about social injustice, sabotage will soon follow.

Movements

Black progress must be stopped at all cost. Any movements that benefit Black people must be sabotaged. WS can't thrive with Black excellence.

They stopped Marcus Garvey's efforts to help Black people return to Africa. J. Edgar Hoover charged Marcus Garvey was charged with mail fraud to prevent Black people from realizing freedom. Although innocent, the charge stopped Garvey's campaign.

Although murder is an extreme way to stop a movement, it is what happened to Dr. Martin Luther King and Malcolm X. However, the most common way to halt a movement is to use money. White supremacists buy off our leaders. Once the Black leader accepts the money, the White supremacist controls the leader.

If White supremacists can not buy the leader, they send in agents to cause friction to destroy the movement. Movements scare the White supremacists because they see it as a threat to their rule.

They know we are the only people that can inspire the nation. Why do you think everyone appropriates what we start? Why do you think they copy everything we do? When we don't stand up for something, it's very noticeable.

Many would say we should fight and I agree with that. The problem is that too many of our people are slave minded and love White people more than they love themselves. People like that don't want liberation but just comfort under WS. They have no problem being at the bottom begging for scraps from WS's table. Many of them are so afraid to even do for self. They will say "White supremacists will destroy us like Black Wall Street if we rebuild that again." They have a genuine fear of what White supremacists *may* do. The cowardice in the Black community is at an all-time high. That's why we are in the horrible condition

that we are in right now. We only fight against each
other. If we fought WS like we fight each other, Black
people would move ahead faster. WS isn't playing
with us, yet we still think it's a game out here.

Chapter 8

The White Supremacist Score Board

The system of WS monitors Black people
twenty-four seven, three sixty-five. Once you realize
how much they monitor us, it will sicken you to the
core. They monitor our speech, fashion, dating
choices, movements, slang, financial spending, etc.
Not one day goes by where WS isn't stalking us.

The quicker the Black community realizes this,
the better off we will be to develop strategies to
combat this issue. The truth is they monitor us because

we're the only group in America that has challenged them and made headway. Although it seems as if we're going backward the potential for that to turn around can happen overnight. The decline of the global European population has made them nervous.

The White supremacist fears that if they become the minority, the atrocities they inflicted on others will be inflicted on them. The Black person's mind is on true freedom; not revenge. Mainstream, White-owned media outlets disseminate propaganda that promotes Blacks as evil people. Factual accounts of the past, American history shows us where evil resides. It shows who is violent, oppressive, and murderous. That's why White supremacists feel we will take revenge on them. They know what they have done to others on this land called America. The fear of retaliation keeps them on guard to keep a scoreboard as a form of control upon Black people. They keep count of us. One Black person represents the entire race yet one White person represents themselves. When a Black person does anything, they will hear about it for the rest of their lives. A White person does something, and society makes excuses for them. The media is the public relations firm for the White male image. The media is used as the bullhorn more than any other entity in America. The purpose of this book is to teach you at a beginner level to see racism and WS. Let's cover how this is done in everyday life.

Jobs

A Black person can't get away with anything on the job. Most Black people would agree with me on this because we have watched the favoritism daily. Black people must stay on task, show up on time every day, can't take extra time at lunch, and have more education or experience than our White counterparts. We have seen our White colleagues try to avoid work, show up late, take extra time at lunch, and have little to no education for the same position. Let me say this with balance so you won't misunderstand me. I don't believe every White person attempts to buck the system nor am I saying every Black person is the model employee. What I'm saying is if a Black person messes up, our managers write us up or even fire us. They do not forgive our screw-up, even those from our teen years and early adult years haunt us, preventing us from gaining employment.

I have watched White guys on jobs mess up and keep their jobs. I remember the one time I messed up on the same job; human resources fired me even though I worked at this company for five years without a single infraction. It doesn't matter if you keep your record clean as a Black person. If you mess up, you're getting suspended or fired.

How many times have we seen unemployed, highly educated Black people? Or, if the Black person is in a decent position, a White person is hired for them to train. In six months, the White person the Black person trained is the supervisor. A Black employee is good enough to train the White person but not to be the supervisor. To add insult to injury, the White person is not as educated as the Black person.

When these issues are brought out in meetings, the collective White team members shun Black people for making problems. Then they will bring up a bunch of old things you did years ago or complain about something current. Current complaints only surface when a Black person seeks to understand why they've been passed over for a position they are experienced and educated to fill. Because of this, I advocate Black entrepreneurship.

When you own your own business, the days of putting up with that kind of treatment are over. The system is set up for Whites to win and for Blacks to fail. I'm not saying we can't overcome the odds because we do that daily. But we as Black people due to our skin color.

Crime

Black on Black crime is a key talking point for White supremacists and their cronies. It helps them to feel good about themselves, maintaining their position of superiority. Most of us know the talking points presented in conservative media platforms. The listeners of those programs repeat the talking points like trained parrots.

- Blacks are 14% of the population yet commit 50% of the murders
- Blacks kill other Blacks in Chicago daily

They deliver these talking points with half-truths. White-owned media does this to indoctrinate society.

They never tell you what created the crime in the Black communities. They never tell you about the drugs placed in those communities. Anyone who knows about the crack epidemic knows cocaine was put in the Black communities by the CIA. Gary Webb exposed this and lost his life for being a true American journalist.

Black communities have no gun manufacturing plants, yet kids in Chicago have talked about finding crates filled with guns and ammo. They don't want to discuss crime.

White supremacists earn money off the deaths of Blacks. Organ traffickers steal the organs of dead Black people and sell them on the Black market. Think about it, if Lil Pookie comes up missing no resources will be set aside to find him. No one cares when Black people go missing. Everyone is in on it--cops, business owners, and elected officials. We wouldn't have crime in the Black community if the White mobs didn't destroy over 200 Black towns. We built those towns with our own hands. Black crime didn't happen until after integration.

White supremacist created the ghetto through a process called redlining. Redlining is "a discriminatory practice by which banks, insurance companies, and other financial institutions refuse or limit loans, mortgages, insurance, and other financial products, within specific geographic areas, especially inner-city neighborhoods." WS created every condition for savage behavior. After introducing ghettos, White supremacists deployed tactics to pull Black men out of homes, effectively breaking up the Black family. As an educated Black man, I refuse to allow them to point the finger at us.

We have never murdered at the level of White people. We've never poisoned nations of people or used biological weapons on anyone. We've never dropped a nuclear bomb on any sovereign nation.

We didn't legalize the murder of children and promoted it as "a woman's right to choose." We aren't the school shooters or lead the nation in pedophilia. Once you start dissecting their crimes, there is no room for them to talk about us.

Their talking points seldom extend beyond robbery and murder. They only focus on what Black people are leading in. Based on their moral authority and high IQs, White supremacist believe they are incapable of committing crimes, using drugs or being savage.

Police Killings

Police involved murders must be stopped. It affects everyone—not just the Black community. But, White supremacists make this about Black people only. It seems to escape them that White people—White children—are killed at the hands of cops as well. However, those cops are, often, brought to justice.

When Black people speak about the deaths of our brothers and sisters, it's an attack on them. They argue more Blacks kill Blacks than cops kill Blacks." They never argue more Whites kill Whites than cops kill Whites." They keep up with the Black victims of police killings only.

During my show, I've had many White people ask, "Why don't the media speak on the Whites that are killed by cops?"

The answer is simple. No one—the powers that be, that is--wants White society to believe that cops indiscriminately kill White people, too. The year 2017 457 Whites were killed by the police. In the same year 223 African Americans were killed by police. If cop killing of Whites were broadcast through media, White people would use their privilege to stop the unjust killings of America citizens. The media knows most people in America don't value Black life so it's ok to show cops killing Black people daily.

Images of dead or murdered Black people enforce WS by normalizing our demise. As long as the media coins police brutality as a Black community issue, we will never resolve it.

White supremacy is imploding on itself because they refuse to address the issues in the White community.

I've heard White people say, "Cops wouldn't kill Black people if you didn't commit crimes." Video after video has surfaced, showing cops escalating incidents with excessive force or racial slurs. For years, the Black community has seen cops who terrorize citizens for no reason or plant drugs on people they don't like. Law enforcement personnel get promotions when they make certain types of arrests. They do it to Black people because the system is against them and they don't have money to defend themselves. The cops know White society is ok with Blacks dying This system is not set up for Back people to win.

WS can only exist by comparing White people to Black people with faulty, inaccurate information. You would think we were the only non-White group in America. For them, Black people are the enemy. They don't view other races enemies because they have not committed the same types of crimes against other races. That's why other races can come to this nation and do well without WS trying to sabotage them every step of the way.

Yes, these other groups are monitored but not the same way the government monitors Black people.

As crazy as it sounds, when Black people push separation or self-segregate, White supremacist cry foul. They must be the ones forcing us to segregate for them to be happy. Anything that we must do against our will makes them happy. The day the Black community wakes up and realizes our power to end our oppression is the day WS dies.

Chapter 9

Blatant Double Standards

Double standards in the system of racism and WS come as a benefit to those with White skin. Non-Whites learn quickly that White people can do or say whatever they want and get away with it. Are White people better than you? No. They benefit from the special privilege of having an excuse made for them no matter what they do.

This system is a creation of White people for White people. This nation's forefathers wrote the founding documents during the enslavement of Black people. Although slavery was abolished in 1865, we struggle on as a people in a country that hates us.

Over the years, we've become educated and attempted to assimilate into their society. However, the majority downplays our successes and broadcast our failures. They magnify our failures to the tenth degree, and we suffer grave consequences. There are no excuses for us.

When a Black person commits a crime, even those with diagnosed mental illnesses, the system takes no pity on us. However, when a White person commits a crime, mental illness is almost always a defense, even when the White person has no history of mental illness. They're given the benefit of the doubt, extended sympathy, and offered multiple chances.

Crime

No matter the group, crime happens in all communities. It's something that we must control. If the US were serious about controlling crime, criminals wouldn't be in authority. This country makes a difference between White crime vs. non-White crime. When the cops arrest a Black male for a drive-by shooting, the media demonizes him. I agree with the demonization because the loss of innocent life is beyond wrong. I want that person to go to prison. However, there are no excuses, not even medical ones, that can intervene on behalf of the Black male. Even when someone accuses a Black male of something, and there is no damaging evidence, we don't see pictures of him on TV smiling or hear his friends saying he was a good person. The Black male is never the victims even when society victimizes him. The Black male is portrayed as the representative of the whole Black race.

When a White male commits a crime, there is always an excuse. We produced a news report of the mass shooting in Las Vegas. A White male by the name of Stephen Paddock killed 58 people and shot over 400 at a concert. The media never called him a terrorist, but if his name had been Tyrone Jones, he would have been called a terrorist. The media gave Stephen Paddock a mental illness cover and sympathetic news reports. The media wanted you to care about him more than the people he killed or injured. He was a devil, yet mainstream media refused to demonize him.

Dylann Roof went into the Emanuel AME Church and killed nine church members. When investigators caught Dylann, the cops took him out to eat. They never called him a terrorist, but if the criminal name were Muhammad Shabazz, then it would be terrorism. The White criminals are never the representatives of their group. The media *always* refers to White mass shooters to as lone wolves. Even though we have a vast history of White criminality, there is always an excuse for that.

Criminal Justice System

The criminal justice system treats White males best. They built the system for our failure and oppression. It's no different at sentencing for crimes committed. The law should treat everyone the same, but it doesn't work that way. Justice is not blind for everyone in the United States. White males have many advantages on their side that favor them. Usually, a White judge presides over a case led by a White, district attorney. You may have non-Whites in those positions, but they can't wield the same punishment against White males as wielded against Black males.

In many cases, the judge knows the families of White criminals. The judge, DA, and jury can sympathize with the White criminal. How many times have we heard cases where judges were beyond lenient? That same judge wouldn't treat Black males in the same manner.

District attorneys seek the maximum punishment for Back men. The judge will never sympathize with a Black male because he doesn't know him or his family. This country teaches all people to hate and distrust Black people. They bring that same hate and distrust to the courtrooms of America.

Black men lead in exonerations in this nation. Our juries are almost always predominantly or all White—especially our secretive grand juries. The one judge that stood against that in his courtroom was Judge Olu Stevens. Judge Stevens is a circuit court judge for the 30th Judicial Circuit, which presides over Jefferson County of Kentucky. He wanted the jury to have a diverse panel. The White DA didn't like that and filed a complaint on the judge. The judge was suspended yet White judges speak up, and nothing happens to them at all. Whites are arrested for 70% of the crimes yet less than half of the prison population. Black men are only 8% of the US population yet represent over 50% of the prison population. According to FBI Uniform Crime Stats, Black people only account for about 24-26% of arrests. The numbers don't add up, do they?

The police are doing their jobs, but the district attorneys and judges allow White criminals to escape jail. Even with Black judges, Black people rarely escape jail.

Everyone knows about the double standard, but no one will confront it. Most in White society is fine with the way Blacks are treated. Why do I say that? They have the power to fix it but stand idly by. Why? They love the benefits of WS.

Employment

Most Black people know that when we have a job, we can't be too vocal about how we feel. We tread lightly because Black people know that raising too many complaints will get you fired or written up.

If Brad or Becky has a problem, they are quite vocal. I have seen this in action and have seen White people go off on their managers with no repercussions. We go along and accept the blatant double standards because we need our jobs. The main reason WS can do this is that we depend on them for way too much. Once we create businesses, we take the power to fire us away. That alone is liberating for any Black person.

Beauty Standards

Black women must deal with being ridiculed on every level when it comes to their overall beauty and style. In the US, blond-haired, blue-eyed Becky is the beauty of standard.

For many years, the full lips, large eyes, and big butts on Black women was ugly, nasty and ghetto. When a White woman wants to inject her lips to resemble the lips of a Black woman, she becomes more beautiful and not ghetto. White women have even resorted to getting butt injections.

Everything that was ugly on a Black woman is now beautiful on White women. When White women do anything, it's the best thing ever. How do you think Black women feel? Don't you think they get tired of White women stealing everything from them? That's why sisters get mad at us brothers when some of us praise White women that bought Black features. A Black girl can be ratchet, and the world clowns her. A White girl like Whoa Vicky can be ratchet and make thousands of dollars a month. If this country judged people fairly, we wouldn't have this issue.

Finance

Whites are given loans and grants at a higher rate than Blacks. Studies show that Whites are given loans at a rate of 32% more than Blacks with the same credit score and financial information. Any Black person that gets into business can tell you how hard it is to grow. Without capital, it's impossible to grow into a viable business.

This country favors Whites for being White.

I'm not writing this to tell Black people to give up. I just want you to be aware of the state of racial affairs in the United States, so we can work collectively to overcome the evil that is before us. We wouldn't need their banks if we pooled our resources together.

One example of resource pooling is when we raised funds to donate to Hurricane Harvey victims. We had a just over 340 people donate a little over $15,000. What if we came together monthly to support or fund black businesses. What if we do that in every city and state? Our liberation is in our hands.

Media

The media covers television, radio, movies, social media, and music. We all know Whites are over-represented in every area. We rarely have anything we can point out as a truly owned Black media. Although Bob Johnson, a Black man, founded BET, he sold it to Viacom. Most of the news outlets are White owned. The record labels are White owned, and the radio stations are White owned. We are shut out in every area, and they take no issue with that.

The social media platforms are White owned, and with Whites promoted more than non-Whites on the various platforms. Facebook allows White supremacists to run amok on the site. A Black person can say support Black-owned businesses and get banned. Yes, that has happened to many people. No matter what, Blacks will always be treated less than. Therefore, it's important for us to create our own media outlets and websites.

They've shown us we're not wanted here, which is why I encourage Black people to obtain a passport and visit African nations. They want us to come to build with them. One of our goals is to establish a major media presence in African nations. Why are we putting up with the double standards that will never change? For the double standards to go away, the system of racism and WS must fall.

In the words of Tupac, "Keep your head up." I know this information is disheartening, but that doesn't mean this system will always prevail. The more we gain an education, run thriving businesses, and support one another, the easier it becomes to defeat

WS. We overcame slavery, Jim Crow, race riots, and crack epidemics. We're a strong and courageous people with the heart of God.

We will overcome this as well!

Conclusion

The manual you just read is intended to get you acclimated to how racism and WS works at a covert level. This book only skims the surface of what's in operation in America. Keep it on your bookshelf as a point of reference and to remind you of the work we must do in the Black community.

Research into how this system works. Many great men and women came before me to break down this system of institutional and perpetual racism. They made it a science. I know as a person that didn't understand a thing about the system a few years ago, but now this person is well-educated and teaches others how to overcome the odds.

After reading this book, pick up works by the master teachers: The Honorable Elijah Muhammad, The Honorable Louis Farrakhan, Dr. Francis Cress Welsing, Neely Fuller, Dr. John Henrik Clarke, Dr. Khalid Muhammad, Malcolm X, Martin Luther King Jr., and Marcus Garvey (Father Of Pan-Africanism).

Don't read this book and forget about it. Encourage others to purchase this book so they can have this information as well.

The greatest con White society pulls on us is to get us to believe WS doesn't exist. If you're a White person that's reading this book and want to make a difference, become unattached from your privilege. Seek equality for your fellow human beings.

If you never attempt to make things right, you are an accomplice. I look forward to working with you to end WS.

What's Next?

A "Woke" Person's Guide to Overcoming WS

I wanted this book to be an instruction manual on identifying PAR in your life. The knowledge in this book shouldn't be stored but used daily to defeat racism and WS. I'm a firm believer in not only complaining but doing something about problems. Remember solutions is what makes change not just identifying a problem. This call to action is something you can do daily to renew your mind from being colonized under the system of WS.

1. Commit to educating yourself in the true history of America.
   a. Remember public schools are meant to indoctrinate you. Education isn't the overall goal.
2. Call out anyone that's being racist or discriminatory.
   a. Learn communication tools, like some of the ones described in this book, to "call out" or challenge in ways that are non-violent and or evoke shame or blame.
3. Encourage friends & family to purchase this book so they can get the knowledge.
4. Obtain a passport. The system doesn't promote world travel. Travel to become a well-rounded person.
5. Register to vote and educated yourself on how to vote on every issue both locally and nationally.

    a. You can't get rid of racist politicians, sheriffs, district attorneys, judges etc. out of office if you don't vote.

6. Practice your 2nd amendment rights. We live in a time where it's dangerous for non-white people. White supremacist groups are attacking innocent people daily. We must protect our family.
7. Teach your children the knowledge you obtained about racism & WS.
8. Prepare yourself to lose friends or family. Some people are comfortable in oppression.
9. Take your first trip to an African nation.
    a. I personally been to Ethiopia and loved it. I suggest start in English speaking countries like Ghana, South Africa, Kenya, Zimbabwe. (Suggestion for African-American readers)
10. Continue to study racism & WS by reading books and listening to messages from our great leaders. Past and Present.

Contact Us

    □   **Bookings/Interviews**

For booking of interviews, speaking engagements or general questions:

kellen@colemanprfirm.com ,
phillipscott@adviseshow.com

- **Watch "The Advise Show" hosted by Author Phil**

  YouTube
  https://youtube.com/TheAdviseShowTV

- **Follow/Start a Chat on Social Media**

  Twitter: https://twitter.com/adviseshowmedia

  Instagram:
  https://instagram.com/advisemedianetwork

  Facebook:
  https://facebook.com/TheAdviseShow

- **Visit Online**

  Website: https://adviseshow.com

Printed in Great Britain
by Amazon

45649883R00069